Nigiste Nigist :
Ancestral, Present & Forever Entangled

Poetic offerings dipped in my personal stash of Blackness.
Truths bumping into & transcending the landscape of Amerikkka.

Written By: ORIT

Nigiste Nigist :
Ancestral, Present & Forever Entangled

Poetic offerings dipped in my personal stash of Blackness.
Truths bumping into & transcending the landscape of Amerikkka

Written By: ORIT

ORIT

Ruach & Emet Publishing

DEDICATIONS

To the **All Encompassing**, the **ONE**, The **GREAT SPIRIT** in every Manifestation, that breathed life into me and purposed this tumultuous journey...

To my Ancestors who are a part of my DNA & Soul whispers; timeless forever's...

To my newest young Ancestor Marshawn McCarrel, a Freedom Warrior with an unparalleled revolutionary heart, who gave up his life for his people to affect change... Your sacrifices were many in life, and I wish you would have felt you didn't have to leave for the next... But until we meet again, I am glad I know peace is your new garment and light heart, your crown.

To those who Love **Mashiach Yeshua**, understand Orisha's, aren't the normal ones, love Ancestral Breaths & sometimes all the above at the same time; finding no contradictions in the bottomless...

To every BLACK Person, especially BLACK Women and Girls, of the Diaspora & Continent, who have been waiting to hear their story confirmed, loved and exalted in the sacred space of truth sharing... I pour myself all out for you... I pour it all out for US.

ACKNOWLEDGMENTS

Marketing Liason: Aiyana Marcus
Graphic Designer: James Engleman, Jr.
Photography: Jennifer Stowers
Make-Up Artist: Melissa Eppinger

The Offerings...

Time is Illusion...

Preface
Warning: Truth Telling Ahead!

ORIT

Preface

Nigiste Nigist is a phrase taken directly from the ancient Abyssinian (Ethiopian) language of Ge'ez. Ge'ez is the mother tongue of many Semitic Languages, including the current and official language of modern Ethiopia:Amharic. Many recognize the word *Negus*, which means "King" in Ge'ez. Naturally, *Nigist* is the feminine version of this word, meaning "Queen."

Notice how Negus/Nigist is so close to *Negro*, derived from *Niger* (Latin), which means Black. Add another "g" to the aforementioned, and you get one of the most well known ethnic slurs on Black People; especially in The Americas. A word that was taken and morphed to oppress, degrade, and badly label Black People... Connotation is everything, for as they called our people *niggers*, and still do so to this day, heinous acts and volatile words are cast upon us, simply because of our beautifully melanin infused skin.

No contradictions here, because Moors and other Africans who conquered Euro & Spanish territories, were royal & advanced peoples... Yes, BLACK is associated with royalty... *Negus, Nigist,* and other terms; all of these have an exalted meaning, which is why white supremacy has made such efforts to make our Blackness: Evil, no good, not to be desired.

Everything started east and worked its way westward. As many know, the oldest remains found of humans have been of BLACK Ethiopians. One of those BLACK Ethiopians found was who European Scientists call "Lucy", and others acknowledge as "Eve." She is the beginning, they believe, of all of us on the planet. It is no wonder, so many African Cultures are influenced, within their own unique paradigm, by the land of Abyssinia.

So Nigiste Nigist literally means " Queen of Kings" or more plainly, a Queen/Woman who rules in her own right. This means that she did not marry to become the ruler of an empire; she ascended the throne just like a man would, or because she was the best for the job. It means her status as woman was not the validating or invalidating factor of her ascension... It wasn't the masculine presence that "made" her. A *Nigiste Nigist* can stand alone in her own power if she so chooses. This is the embodiment of who I am, and many other BLACK Women as well.

For a considerable number of BLACK Women in Feminist & Womanist circles, being called a "queen" has become synonymous with BLACK Men who have a misogynoir mindset. Men who want to call us queens, and then rule over us, and demean our power to become and be and do. A way to put chains, where we should be free... A way to practice the form of patriarchy that was brought to our conscious by European enslavers and land nabber's, under the complicated guise of being"woke."

I've personally decided, that I will not allow the misguided and obtuse, to stop me from remembering... Remembering that the ancient, and not so ancient rulers of various nations of Africa, were fierce warrior women. Strategists, highly intelligent, powerfully feminine, rightfully cut throat and measured, nation savers and makers: Goddesses! They were not weak, and they were, in most cases, not prohibited from using their talents based off their blessed status as women. They were respected, and they were revered because of their capabilities.

Black Women, we have all of this and more in us still today... It is in our DNA. I find that *Nigiste Nigist,* queen, empress, or any other royal designation; they are terms of empowerment and remembrance to me, though I do understand and respect some women feel some sort of way about such terms. To me, they exemplify the amazing Divine nature of BLACK Women, showing our ability to be and do everything; including the sacred rites that only we are immersed in.

I do not see it as a hierarchy of you ruling over me and vice versa. I do, however, understand that royals had an exalted position over the people throughout history. I see royal titles, in our collective case whilst shipwrecked on these Amerikkkan shores, in terms of the exalted honor we have as the originators of all humans... A collective governing that requires us to not only reclaim, but to responsibly take charge and lead in truth and integrity. After all, Patriarchy as we know it today, is new to African Peoples in the scope of history's time continuum.

When we as Black People of variance, are experiencing so much hatred based on who we are, reminding ourselves about our "highness", as Queens and Kings **in the right context**, can be very soothing to our soul health. I believe that it invokes remembrance... Truth... Helps us keep going and keep our heads in the high position that they should have never been lowered from.

Being exiled here in our now home Amerikkka, is definitely interesting. We live here... We're use to being here, but our heartbeat cadence and our soul rhythms tell us we are not home, well at least that is how I feel, how about you? Our Ancestors, with their highly educated and royal-esque ways were enslaved and brought to work these stolen lands. This hurt is still in our DNA, and the hatred of the enslaver is still in the DNA of those who continue, by choice, to propagate the systematic hatred, that bridles our souls from speaking clearly and authentically.

WARNING: TRUTH TELLING AHEAD

Hey everybody!

I am excited for you to enter this poetic offering, expressed through my lens, my soul. I need you all to keep a few things in mind when reading this body of work.

The first thing is, this is a completely honest collection of life. I do not hold my thoughts in, I use strong language at times, and I elaborate about the happenings Black People face in Amerikkka, blatantly. I do not subscribe to words being "curses" in themselves, nor do I think that it affects my Spirituality. I believe that the way in which you use any word has the power to bless or curse. I do not apologize for my honesty, but I do, as a courtesy, want to extend you this warm warning... Just in case naked honesty is not your thing, you can't say you weren't warned.

I do not use words that people designate as profanity too much, actually not very often, but it is present in its appropriate spaces throughout my various prose pieces. They are deliberate and important to the truth. They are not any more present, perhaps even less present, than any movie or song you allow your kids to listen to nowadays. Having said that, I think that every parent or educator, has the right to decide what material those in your charge are ready for. There is **triggering subject matter within,** because oppression and violence is a real life thing. Again, for those who are sensitive to certain word usage, you can thereby prepare yourself by this warning. There are messages about every aspect of life in this poetic work... Life is nuance... Life is real.

The next thing I would like all of you to keep in mind as we journey together, is that it is important when you are reading each piece, not to assume you know where I am going until the very end of that said piece. I most definitely and defiantly will challenge you, with the sweat of truth in my poetry. You sometimes, may want to turn away because I hit a spot that is uncomfortable here and there. I have personally found that transcendence happens by crossing the bridges of the unknown, and decidedly walking over the hot coals that make us more honest. If you are truly wanting to understand and take in the *Set-Apart Energy*; take your time, breathe, and complete each piece thoughtfully.

Lastly, I want you to feel free to BE, as you read this definitive collection of poetry. Black People, I want you to know that these words written are for you, even in the midst of my personal storytelling. You are allowed to expand, and you have permission to feel everything... Relate it to your life as you see fit, look within when you are ready, and find the courage to be real in the places you need to be... Transforming into more of who you really are.

You are welcome here, no matter who you are. I hope other folks who are not Black will read these pages, and get a glimpse of what it's like from a Black Woman of nuance perspective in Amerikkka. I want to invite you to engage this prose thoughtfully, but not to tear it apart as an outsider. You are a welcomed guest, but this feast is not being held in your honor, with your tastes in consideration. Therefore, the menu items and the fanfare will be foreign to you. Respect this, and I hope you will transform & give space to honesty as you read along... Giving room for the holy space of solemnity, of an experience you live outside of.... Respect Respect Respect this!

I am humbled you are about to partake of this poetic journey with me. Dig in!

1.
Misogynoir

I'm not just woman, I am Wombman... Originator of all life... Of even you white ones who hate this fact; especially white men. Erasing the truth of our Divineness at every chance you get. Original flows like a sacred solemnity kept in my sacred rivers, anointed in the startling reverberation of deeply alluring BLACKNESS. Goddess? I am Goddess-She is Goddess-WE are Goddess. So every time my brown sisters and I have our beautiful skin, our beautiful quick and creative minds, our beautiful innovation without compromise, our beautiful crowns you call hair, and our beautiful bubble butts you like to stare... AT...

Maligned-Denied-Ridiculed-Silenced-Erased... Trying to convince us that our unique allure, should be replaced... Replaced with European everything, or so you say. Erasing us from the history that tells our stories.... Stealing our glory, to cover and legitimatize your shame. You tell us, through control of mediums & image creators bare, that your woman...Her pale skin and essence, is what is truly fair. Centuries old mind games and tricks... Lies, deceit, a total miss...

You say BLACK woman is a wildebeest, a witch, a conjurer with a seductive stare. Even our men, too many BLACK men, join in your dangerous game. A contagious pathogen released during the play... Killing souls, sacred space, timeless forevers.

You make fun of us, jesting behind our backs, yet every fantasy in your clandestine minds eye... Is wrapped in beautifully bold mahogany limbs embrace; we have always been the object of your desire. Whether slave or free, BLACK women have always made you succumb to all the things you say make us...Ugly.

You love to fuck us... Never at a loss for a splatter that mixed in our cake batter... Diversifying our blackness; Sacred solemnity still kept. All the while through rape, torture, and unwanted advances of you... You who said we were: Too dumb, Too dark, Too animal like, Too unworthy. Not an image of desire... You, sir, are a mother fucking liar!

Every time I see you invent ways to paint your pale woman's skin my shade... Through lotions, machines, & bronzer's. Every time you pay a plastic surgeon to give your supposed object of desire: My lips, My hips, My butt, My eye size... I laugh, I pause, I sigh.

When some BLACK Men follow your lead, sequestering love for Black Women in colorism and self hates broken row boat, on colonialism's ocean deep... Telling me and my sisters that we are: Too BLACK, Too strong, Too smart mouthed, Too reminiscent of Africa. These same sick ones say that BLACK Wombman has always been: Too ratchet, Too ghetto, Too loud, Too demanding.

End play, by the end of the game, too many Goddesses try to live in the liars web; seeking to soften self esteem shattering. White women are everything we're not... So you say... But even the BLACK Men who says BLACK Women are trash, want his white woman to have some ass and sass... Reminders of home found deep in our wells, parched by rejection-hurt-shame.

I am not just woman, I am Wombman... Original runs through my veins. I am Goddess, she is Goddess, my sisters and I are equally Divine, dipped in variable BLACKNESS. Our royal garment is melanin, and our kinky hair our jeweled crown. Our power is unnerving, we command the room, unintentionally, to your dismay.

Keep lying by saying, we are nothing to you when we have been your greatest inspiration... Your sure and steady footstool to your ill-gotten facade of greatness. Your secret is known, your attempts to subdue realized... Now BLACK Wombmen must build ourselves up, and take our royal place... Rise!

Beloved by the CREATOR, and anointed by the SUN. Remarkably hated by many in male space of whose journey we've guided into existence. Yet, we will continue to cradle all that is, orbit everything that will be, actualize holy realities.

Why would we? Why should we? Why can we? Keep pressing? Cause' Greatness is what we're made of... Nothing can be sustained without us, nothing can exist without our exhalations; our life giving deep breaths.

2.
Misconceptions Conception

Jealousy, Hatred, and Lies had Ménage à Trois
It was dirty, painful, and shook the entire earth
Lies got pregnant by them both,
Neither Jealousy or Hatred pulled out
A baby made by three, would soon unbalance the entire earth.

They begged Lies to abort,
afraid of what the consequences would be...
But lies deceived them both,
and carried the baby, hiding it in its mouth.

Misconception was born, to the others dismay,
who they vowed that day, to never claim...
A mean little thing from the start, perhaps aware of the
abandonment and dark hearts that conceived it.

Neither male or female, no distinction, blurred lines,
Resenting its being, seeing, feeling... Being alive.
As Misconception began to grow up, the colder it became
Never able to be kind, casting its shade on first meeting to all,
whom it blamed.

Never understanding, unable from the very start...
The offspring of Jealousy, Hatred, and Lies was being its innate
self; without compromise. A cold and dark creation undone... And
it grew and grew and grew...

Misconception is full grown now, and wreaking havoc all the time.
Starting wars, causing rifts, making folk angry, shutting folks out.
Perhaps we can help Misconception to be free, from its repulsive
ways, its indignity... But Misconception would have to want to
choose a new course, a new way...

Just like we must choose to not heed its slander.
After all, Misconception only feeds off our desire for its Jealousy,
Hatred and Lies... Its DNA is alive, in our willingness to
compromise.

3.
Ancient Rememebrance

It's in the familiarity certain hues in the sky sing to my restless longing. My soul wells up, only sometimes, I have never considered why until this very moment...

Listening with my eye, a cloud felt, a light ray heard before...
I zone out into my holy space without worry, dogma, or form. It's in that moment, quick as a flash, when the winds remind me of an all inclusive past...

A spicy and sweet aroma travels in the air, soul inhales deeply, my heart skips quickly... What is this that makes my energy centers gleam intensely? I do not dare... Question too analytically, in a sweet moment, a part of me... Older than me… Mesmerizing intoxication; reassuring my safe passage...I breathe truest.

It's in the connection of our eyes, when soul realizes, I am looking at the DIVINE! Frighteningly familiar, I dare not turn away... The truth lay, in the windows of your heart. I need to peer deeply through your glass... Smudges present, clear and true your imperfection; I see clearly.

It's in the wisdom that boils up from my unknown... Bottomless-Limitless-HOME... Ancestral song, present course, future journey... My choice? Calling me, healing me, loving me... This assuring that I remember... A glimpse of all of me.

4.
Prentis

One day has come, and no I can't unblock you from my phone. I warned you for four years, you can't share air with me now: I've cried too many tears. I gave you room to mourn the child in you who never had a toy, you toyed with me instead... My fault, I know.

Anointed by patriarchy and confirmed by Black Jewishness; I thought I had to be the prettiest rug you had ever walked upon. I let you wipe your dirty soiled feet on me, happily... What the hell was wrong with me? Was blind, but now I see... I see that G-D doesn't want woman to die so that man can live.

I gave you a part of my soul, that you misplaced somewhere in the omniverse... Like, I want that shit back... I don't want you to find it though... I'll do that myself! Typically careless of your dealings with me... I was so blind, but now I see... How could I have not seen before?

And furthermore... When I was in a tough spot, unbelievably bad turn of events suffocating me like *Job*... You let me sleep in my car in the dead of winter... Fear and unknown surrounding me. You knew and didn't flinch when I told you on the phone, that I was so cold... Oh, so cold.

I shutter at the remembrance... Seizure from starvation, close to my death.... But your overbearing Bishop, had you in walking dead trance. You didn't want to lose his favor, what an absolute mess! But you care about me... I am so special to you, right? Glad I found YAH's Light and lifted myself out of the dark of that night.

Sorry? "I'm sorry" is what you said when I was again thriving... So you say, so you say, is why you are still guilty to this very day. I had given you so much from my reservoir, beautiful choice things that could sustain our progeny's progeny, undoubtedly. The only solace I have is you never got to taste this Divine-esque Punani, dipped in regenerating *noir*, choice fruit you'll always wonder about... The place the fountain of youth goes to purify itself. Life sustaining warmth... A resting place kept away from your undeserving ass. In this, I'm truly blessed.

You were not worthy of my love, my concern, my heart toward you... You decided that you would misuse and abuse... My loyalty sheltered you, as you caused unholy dissimulation within me... I stayed, MY FAULT, I take that responsibility...

I kept allowing you in. Insult after insult... Lie after lie... I was here first and didn't realize, but you had two lives going on at the same time... Even proposed to another woman, but when that died, that mirage fizzled before your eyes, you wanted to come home, to the one who always loved you. But when you saw I was through, you went back to her... If only she knew, boy if she knew!

I hope you have changed for her... If you haven't I really feel sorry for her... Does she know your certainty about her, was based off my warrior stance of no more? Finally, after I saw you were not just misunderstood, but truly evil and unkind... I allowed the *listening* to guide me and that is why you can't reach me... It's far too late, night has turned to day... Finally!

I've seen your texts in my phones filter, and you are still arrogant as ever... Lying, trying to trick me into having intellectual intercourse with you, but never! Never again will you be graced to have me in your life... No longer will I be there to take care of you, and heal your insistent wounds...

So, stop trying to call- Don't text- Don't send snail mail... You're erased! Cause' this welcome rug has turned into warning signs... No Trespassing! Beware! Unauthorized Persons, Keep Out!

5.
Old Soul, New Life

Ancient scripts plastered on my laptop screen
Telling me how to truly be free and fly higher
Lavender, mint, incense vapors ingesting
As a movie playing in my background watches over me...
Watches as I pluck my eyebrows like Nefertiti...

Not much has changed and yet everything is different.
Gentle impressions... My dark brown eyes eerily reflect blue gaze
For a moment, for a second, others gasp... Is it really that
frightening? I guess!

In full color... In HD in fact, I see black & white sepia splashes of
the past. Inward grown, from childhood began
Seeing the deepest part of every woman and man
Longing for the smell of rain, for gloomy skies
Jazzy-Sexy-Nights.

A mothering insight all my life, never a child free to roam
Whispers of a certain type of song, that only the elders know... I
hum along, though not ready to sing the song. Aware of my shell, I
sit quietly and sip on my smoothie... Strumming my ten stringed
harp, and tweeting profusely.

6.
ORI

Light, Torah, Essential part of the Soul,
the most holy sanctum, in direct
correspondence with the CREATOR.

Three directions of African Ancient Psalm...
SPIRIT walks in the cool of the day
guiding me, Ashe', through every dispensation... Every way.
Every realm rendering me open.

Refusal to trespass, answer destiny with wilderness bare
with every danger and snare.
Ascension propels steady resolve...
Just scratching the surface... Memory.

7.
BUDA (Possessor of the Evil Eye)

Dressed in white, priestly garb, untouched, dark brown,
skin perfect, lean frame, humble eyes... Divine mark unseen,
but felt immensely; poignant gaze lovingly starring...
Beckoning: Be my friend?

But jealousy, misappropriating Solomon & Sheba Dynasty;
A royalty unbending, is the sad reality. The howl of the hyena in
the cool of the night sky... Your reason to lie, your reason to chide,
your reason to debase and connive.

Those eyes, so warm, so true, would do anything for you; but
betrayal, your betrayal... Convincing all that these ones dressed in
white are appalling, degenerate, not one of you: OUTSIDER!

Beautiful hearts and tender souls, head cast down, shame;
drowning in centuries old tears. Freedom, oh freedom... Freedom
over we? From afar, from times past and present, this hurts me
deeply.

Knowing half of me is enslaved in other lands, while I struggle to
breathe in Amerikkka, the land of sour milk and poisoned honey. I
shutter, we shutter... Do our lives have meaning? Are we just
some sick joke... A perpetual reproach? Wanting to be all I can be,
sad my people escaped one hell to be in another...

Ha'aretz is not what it was supposed to be... Tears still flowing...
There and here, anywhere and everywhere we are.
Times three... Every part of me has been dipped in Ancestral
Captivity... All three directions... Being alive, being in this present
order of "time..." The hatred caused by white supremacy's lies, still
doesn't subside... Trickling down to brown on brown crimes of the
heart and flesh... Pain global, pain haunting.

Buda, we're buda? I swear I can't fucking breathe... Escaping one hell, to arrive in another, my family the buda.... Oh buda, evil eye all over we. And before I be a slave, I'd be buried in my grave... Why are these evil eyes, all over we.

I just want all of me, every African part of me, oneness are WE, to be free... I want my people free! We are not possessor of the evil eye, or beholders of magic to transform... We are adorned from on HIGH, the hate in your eyes, is the only evil we've ever known.

8.
The Hair Lies I Tell

When I was a young ebony girl, with big bold eyes and features unfamiliar to the black folk I knew... I was told, by other young ones, little black boys especially, that I was ugly... Weird looking. I wasn't pretty to them, and I was too skinny with no boobs... And on top of all this, I had to be tall too?

The only physical thing, that everyone agreed, was my beautiful hair made me "almost" pretty. When my hair would be pressed and hang down to my behind, everyone would say I was gorgeous... Finally Lovely in their eyes.

When my hair was in it's natural state, everyone would remark that I had "good hair"... Acceptability... It made me feel accepted... Like, I was in living color, finally alive to them! My imaginary "ugliness", constructed by others, wasn't seen for that moment in time. I felt that my hair was my only something, the only thing I had, that made me not the object of scorn.

I didn't realize that my outward beauty was there... I didn't care about my inward beauty, my best feature, because no one else seemed to care. I based my worth around the illusions of others; dipped in systematic racism's sea of lies... We all dived sharply, perpetually blinded by the normality, of its salty waters lukewarm and burning.

I've grown since then, thank G-D! A woman, with strong **B**lack pride and sense of self. I grew into my features, and realized they were indeed beautiful. My hair I love... Kinky, wavy, curly in the lower back side... But here is the thing... The honest and truest truth; I hide from me, from you, deep down inside...

I care too much, and I am a little too happy that my hair finely spirals on its own... That the kink present doesn't disturb this flow.

I don't admit it to myself usually, but I still, somewhere deep down, think my hair is my best thing... The main thing, that makes me more than "bearable" to look at.

Would I feel as good if my hair were a little more kinkier? After all, When I was little, my hair got labeled... As the only something about me, that made me bearable. Residual sickness hidden? A speck still there? Not totally delivered?

Would I feel just as gorgeous if my kinks were tighter, with no pattern that twirls and fly's? Oppressors lies leaving a salty water stain on my poignant **B**lack Pride... I sigh. I say it wouldn't matter, if my hair didn't twirl and fly organically... Not to say its all that loose now... BUT if my hair were different than my actuality, would I still be filled with the same kinky hair pride?I admit, I don't know. Residual sickness hidden? A speck still there? Not totally delivered?

I say yes of course, because that is how I should feel, but I lie... Deep down, I know I have some hurt, some sickness on the inside. To the bottom of that salty sea... I must dive, to reclaim that bit of myself, the part of myself, I have allowed to drown in the lies of other people's mirages.

I've always gawked in awe, of beautifully 4C kinky mane... It always seemed those wearing it were more gorgeous, sensual, divine highness, breath taking than I could ever be... But not on me? I couldn't see, that this would look good on me... Let's just be honest... It doesn't make sense, but neither does the salty waves of delusions injustice... Residual sickness hidden? A speck still there? Not totally delivered?

"I don't think I would be able to "pull off" kinkier hair than what I have now", I've said to myself... My face isn't as pretty as theirs, I've lamented wrongly... Yes, these thoughts have actually crossed my mind. I rebuked the thought immediately, but I must share the deepest hidden things inside of me, because I am committed to FREEDOM; Freedom starts within me!

When people say they wish they had hair like mine, I scold them and tell them how gorgeous they are... I truly believe they are, I really do! It's just that... Residual sickness hidden? A speck still there? Not totally delivered?

I feel my eyes are too much, though gorgeous, my nose is too strange, yet perfect, my forehead too Horn of Africa, whilst becoming... Traits I had to learn were not ugly. Yet and still, I have an issue with my hair texture... Am I all the way well from my sea sickness? Yes, that is the question of questions.

Let's just be honest... I was told my hair was the only thing that was pretty about me as a child... The supposed best part of me. Though I know it's not true mentally, and see the beauty of all Black Hair in its variation, I still think it would make me... Just me, ugly, because of my earlier impressions. Though I should want to be nothing but what I am, the idea that something as trivial as my hair, could have such an effect on what makes me attractive in my own minds eye, is disturbing & must be undone.

Don't try to twist my words in this honesty session, or think I mean but what I say... I am showing you the complexity of non-mixable realities... Continually being stirred... Never becoming one. All of what I say on this is true, and I know I am not the only one...

We are all complex beings of strength and lack... Full grown and immature... Proud and ashamed. I think people who are pretty, attractive to the visual eye; their hair doesn't matter. Yet, my subconscious taunts my conscious in the real reality.

So yes, when hair compliments and unethical comparisons come in my favor... I secretly feel happy I can be pretty in some way... That I have something they want... This is sick, I am embarrassed to say, but it's true. See how fucked up that is? It's just hair, dear G-D it's just hair!

I confess, this is a mess... I am ashamed to admit, but I do. I know someone else understands this sickness of self hate, from colonialism's influence and waves, on the dirtiest ocean never blue...

Residual sickness hidden? A speck still there? Not totally delivered? Nope, not yet! Learned and infused daily; corrupts wholly...Totally... This is why I have vowed to decolonize my mind daily.

By the time you read or hear this poem, I may have totally gotten rid of this malady. Being honest in this moment, admitting I struggle, whilst a woman of staunch Black Warrior Stance... Yes, this honesty is so very important! I am not done evolving, and that's okay, as long as I keep growing and growing and growing...

I am not my hair, not my frame, not my weight... I am so beautiful inside & that should be my center. I still have work to do, I know I am not the only one... Honesty in this prose means half the battle is won... And the hair lies I tell... Good things about me I should believe; will certainly manifest completely, if I keep being honest with me.

9.
Come On (Aunt Bea)

You called my name, I remember it well. I missed you, I needed you... Hadn't yet misplaced the aroma, of your sweet smell. You came to me, I know you did, our bond broken never. Right then and dream world collide, in strong yet smooth cocktail; spirits...

You called out my name, you were on the scene, my heroine, my everything. Your presence always brought so much relief, so much peace, I could breathe again... It was okay now.

This time you were especially needed, it had been two weeks, I was so happy you hadn't really left me; all encompassing relief... Or so it seemed, or so it seemed.

You called my name,and told me to "come on!"
Break with mold, dream form, vision drop, or merge of the two? I dunno! Stripped of the blending of realms, I looked around, you were gone, how could I go with you... Like you asked me to?

Despair, the greatest unnerving... The realization of chasms illustrious stare- Beckoning the longing, moaning back in my reality... Deeply, deeply I wept, sacred perplexities, afraid of my sight... What were you trying to tell me? Are you gone for good? I'm unfamiliar in this new fear of you... You who loved me best.

Not knowing another soul who would understand, I never could make sense of it all myself. I kept this in my heart, 11 years old at the time, my soul still cries at 32. I think of it quite often even now; our last visit... My last chance?

What was it I didn't quite get? I would've done anything to stay with you; my home. I still don't know what it means... But one day I will, for now the best I can say, from my heart to yours is: I miss you, Aunt Bea. One day, I'll come on... But for now, I'll keep going strong, where I am, how I am. Your hearts song eternally, keeps my soul singing resiliently, until we meet again on the next leg of new life's journey. Ashe'!

10.
Cadence

Unrelenting heart
Perpetual break solid
Purest offering

Knowing sacrifice
Selfish gusts unsteadiness
Balance through Aje'

Uplift the humble
Winnowed freedom flames BURNING
Inferno sustained

11.
To Be Pretty

Every flaw, yes them all, when I welcome them in my spaces...
Kept and unkept, the most holy of sacred realities glistening.
Every stretch mark, every dark mark, every birth mark, every
indent. This is my true pretty... Where all my real pretty is kept.

Prickly legs, eyebrows *un-fleeked*, don't even try to be surprised...
No charcoal lined eyes, that incite ancient, present, and future
alluring... I stayed up all night long searching truth, dismantling the
systems lies on my mind. Cause This is my true pretty... Were all
my real pretty is kept.

Plans for our freedom, plans to disrupt, fragility of non-melanin
kind... Didn't allow me to get my hair just so, at least it's not in my
3rd EYE. A little lip gloss and the anointing of blackness will suit
me just fine, it's fine! Cause' This is my true pretty... Where all my
real pretty is kept.

When dolled up like Black Barbie, intricate care paid to each detail
of mine. Everything in its place, shine, dazzle... Feelin' good,
lookin' fine! I know I'm undone until I look inside, and get some of
my pretty, what really makes me a dime...Cause...

My pretty is authenticity, My pretty is natural and undone.
My pretty stands up for Justice; unwavering until the battle is won.
My pretty loves her body, my pretty embraces each flaw.
My pretty doesn't believe the hype that the media likes to throw on
the proverbial wall. My pretty swings high tide, My pretty swings
low stream. I take my pretty with me everywhere, no matter how
hard it may be.

My pretty isn't made of coiffed hair and elegant dress, or big
alluring eyes... My heart, My soul, My opened SPIRIT eye, my
mind, my high vibe... That's where my pretty resides-

Yes, this is my true pretty, where all my real pretty… Sight into true reality, this is where my pretty is kept.

12.
Fluid

The wind is cool, the waters are warm... Energizing this intoxicating storm. Violently soft... Disturbingly fresh, assured, steady, and ready.

Your intense flow, readying me... Splashing to and fro blissfully; we collide precise and unpracticed. Giving into forbidden wiles, to the surface they rise... There is no turning back; deeply immersed scattering.

The truth of undiscovered waters flow freely, with the steady known streams I mainly go... Oh, but to flow freely, to allow this storm to bellow and roar, to not quell calm, to not deny... Soul knows, soul is quiet, in the transference of this higher reality... Truest to you, truest to me...

Every part of us rolling-flowing-growing-deeply.
I can't deny the winds blow from each side, clashing in warm waters and making travel true. This is how we came to be, a rare poignant journey...

Forceful metering, distance made... Disturbed by the perfect flow, I wonder how I got here, but I need not know... I am safe in these crashing bellows of you- My uncertain certainty; divine perplexity.

Arabesque our design, layers of beauty intertwined... It dare not compromise, this truthful ambiguity. All of me and you, soul to soul... Defined most pure in ancient tomorrows calm. Known streams still flow truest, fresh waters free to pass close by, if it decides... If it decides.

13.
Puty-Tang Blues

I want my back blown out too, boo boo... Just as much as you do.
But I have no room to store, I must protectively an actively abhor,
The muddying of my energy's sacral complexities.
It gotta be just right, it gotta be so true...
And this is why I got, these Puty-Tang Blues.

5 years without exchange, I sorely don't recommend it.
The urge to merge is natural, sensual, steadying and quite sacred.
Rolling deeply in choice waters solely,
whole self in tact is the goal.
No time for fools, Too damn much to lose
And this is why I got these Puty-Tang Blues.

Not prudish or ever ashamed of my carnal splishes and splashes.
Devoutly limitless, appropriate impropriety, sensual solemnity is
kept. Aware my choice streams, solely over choice landscape,
at their peak time and season.
My heart's rules, I ain't no fool
And Yet I still got these Puty-Tang Blues.

Woman free to be... No curse! *Femme Fatale*, blessings
surrounding. I am quite aware of my power and strength, when
high transference rests. So frustratingly perfect, so vital, so
needed to be brought to the truest of true.
Understood by few, very few catch the cue
And this is why I got these Puty-Tang Blues.

14.
Womb

Giver of life, given from on high
Touch the sky, touch the workings lining... G-D rests.

Giver of peoples, nations, lands
Touch the ocean floor, touch the cord... G-D speaks.

Giver of cultures, tongues, purposes, paths
Touch the ground, seed of vital found... G-D manifests.

15.
Phone Voice

The respect I receive, when I cancel the melanin in my voice timbre... The ancient from my tongue. A betrayal of ancestral gusts that blow impatiently in my soul, every heart chamber perplexed. So natural to do, reinforced in school by oppressors standards & conditions of being "the best..."

Their best, not ours. Without even thinking, my tall lean frame, with luscious dark brown skin, my curly kinky hair I wear as a crown of consciousness... All these cast aside, for those moments in time, when I subconsciously dive into my phone voice.

Wanting easy passage, being short on time, knowing the beautiful Blackness in my voice doesn't allow me to get what is mine... Great customer care, or respect of my intelligence... My phone voice tells my soul lies, that I brush off with survival and need for efficiency. Even though my name is not American as apple pie, I still can hide behind the obscurity of ambiguity... They won't write me off immediately, if I use my phone voice.

It truly never occurred to me, not even when I jest with other Black Folks... That we never question, or hold each other up under truth's glare, when it comes to, phone voice... An unspoken understanding of oppressed African Beings... Succumbing to this systems reeling's and heeding's...

We don't even blink when we "put on"... Why is it so easy? Even with all of our collective Black Pride... I feel sick inside. In reality, the centuries old damage done, is only beginning to be known-DNA carries. Whilst those unaffected by privileged blinded eyes, continue to live freely-Completely lacking empathy.

My phone voice is accepted as the "intelligence" that systematic lies boasts as true... That being freed of the beautiful dialectical language(s) we have created in captivity, is progress. We are taught to take the sass and rhythm out of our words... How G-D sounds! Melanated resonance not to be heard, to be something lower than ourselves... To be accepted.

When we overcome these lies, and reject subconscious auto-play... Living to see another day and be self-determining... Then we will rise! We will speak colorfully... Not afraid to fight for our due respect and dignity.

Our brilliance is lofty... It sits on high, never ever should have been reduced to oppressors lies... So, speak melanin, internal drumbeat pulsate my every word... Honestly I stand, however I truly am... No more putting on or disguises. I am, we are... Worthy to be.

16.
Say My Whole Damn Name!

You say your curious... You say it's pretty, but why is your nose turned up and your eyebrow raised ?! You want to know my back story, or so you say, but your smirk and dismissive tone call you liar to my face.

You are nosy, demanding, lacking respect... Not because you inquire, but because you want to play shape-shifter... Thinking I don't see your real goal, and that it's amiss! It's not yourself you want to rearrange, unfortunately... You want how you see me to be a certain way, and you want me to re-shape my self view, around the comfort you find in your perceptions... How quaint.

You push and prod so you can squeeze me... So I can fit nicely into one of the standard size boxes you've intrinsically placed, in the lower attic ,of your cobweb infested mind... Le sigh!

This is your dream, not mine... I live the nightmare of white gaze and melanin-less expectations that you perpetrate on me; playing footsie with my name... The name by which I answer to... Who I AM.

Ah, yes... That... Your one of those. You want to pretend to be chummy with me to disengage my soul rhythms, and the cadence of my heartbeat. Wanting me, my name, my identity to assimilate to yours... Something of which you can relate and then misappropriate. White supremacy has made you lazy... Yes YOU... L-A-Z-Y!

After all, this is Amerikkka... Made into being by the genocide of the indigenous, and the genocide & torturous work of Africans made slaves. Your unspoken words are loudest in the held back honesty you think I am too simple to realize... Too numb to feel... Too... You don't even consider I can see you. Your clearest and most true reality; highest disrespect... This expectation of conformity into a lesser god... Into your image.

After your smirks and halfhearted inquires, you decide you'll give me a "new name", of your liking... To make it easier for YOU, of course. Oh, I love nicknames from those who know me... Those who are intimately intertwined with me, those with whom I grant the ease of chummy...But that isn't who you are... You know it, I know it.

You just don't want to have to deal with my name. My name is poignant and reminds you that your world, your thoughts, your ways were not considered in its making. You pretend renaming me for your ease, is a friendly gesture... A way to become "familiar..."

When truly your intention is to make me palatable to the hunger of your unease... Folks like you... Your stench precedes you, from a long distance away. I used to pretend to not see, to not smell the stench of unauthentic in the moldy crisp air that blows about you, and those like you, but I grew from that place... And what a growth spurt it was!

Now when I'm around you, and you're around me... I will insist you say my whole damn name... Correct you every time you get it wrong... For way too long i've eclipsed when I should be fully visible and strong... And you will learn and go along with my stance, or avoid me all together... Choose!

17.
The Ancestors Aren't Pleased!

Nonliving winds and stale leaves still on the trees,
Tell me indeed, the Ancestors are not pleased.
Monarch butterfly's tapestry sullen, faded, bland...
They tell that the Ancestors, simply cannot understand...
Why we have forgotten, to mark their ways and sayings?
Why we have neglected to listen, to breathe, to live rightly?
Why we have few elders, reaching their hand in hand with their
progeny drowning? Why we do not help our sister or brother,
when we see them perpetually falling?

Waters once cool, now lukewarm and stagnant, tell me the
Ancestors hearts have been saddened. Rich earth of mineral
hopes, dreams now shattered, tell me the Ancestors would still
like to matter... But we are too busy, living of and for ourselves
always. But we are too smitten and filled, with the partial
knowledge of folly's trespass. But we are too quick to discount, the
Divine and vibe so much higher. But we are unaware or refuse to
KNOW, that G-D indeed dwells on our inside.

Thunder and lightning disobedient to their station, Revealing the
Ancestors are in fervent litigation. Winter in Summer and Spring in
Autumn, tells us the Ancestors are ready to offer...
Guidance from the ONE who made us all, our CREATOR.
Guidance from the Aerial view, so we can thrive and get further.
Guidance to get to the realm where we can one day rest, with
them happily. Guidance beating on our internal drum...
Just listen... Listen... Cadence---- unnerving.

18.
Offering

Smoke tastes sweet in the sight of the nostrils lips...
There is no beginning and there is no ending, if true.
Savors-Resin-Heartbeat-Blood…
Transposes the intensity of love...
Sacrifice complete in the truth of my souls intention,
in your honor I bow in obeisance.
Will this please you? Will you receive it?

19.
New Black

Mirage is your house number and deception is your zip code...
Brand new you, accepted by the abominable, congrats! You got
out the hood and tied your hands behind your back, turning away
to partake of the preferred drink of faux comfort and choice
compromise...

Never looking back, purposely forgetting to remember; your
amnesia isn't real. You can't be real anymore, the soul price you
pay... Too arrogant to realize we can see you... We know you.

And then there's you, Ms. or Mr. "Never lived in the hood", poor
people your worst fear... That they may cross your path and
disrupt the elusive continuity, of the the semblance of ease, that
precedes you... The mirage you were born into.

Unable to see yourself as you truly are, you have defined yourself
by Gucci, Prada, and that exclusive Black Centurion Card... You
hold your breaths, our breaths, so that your blood can seem
blue... It will never be, no matter how much you lie to you...

You, both of your types, are still the power of our Ancestors hopes
and fears all at the same damn time... I mean to disturb you... I
mean to shake you where you sleep walk daily. I mean to tell you
that your new *frenemies* laugh at you behind your back, while
perpetually I sigh... Wondering-Thinking-Disconcerting... Why
continue to lie... To yourself?

I have come, oh so close, to cursing your existence... But then
chastisement from inside lays me bare in my own unbalanced
superiority remembering... Remembering I had to grow, I am
growing still.

There is breath we share, that binds us... You may not like it, I may not like it, but it lays bare in our most naked showing. Time is shape shifting and the reality of where we are is soon to disrupt perceptions unsteady... You and me, and the rest of us are still WE. Baby, You still BLACK... Just/ like/ me.

20.
The Gas
(To the Tune of "The Star Spangled Banner")

And rockets coral tint glare
Releasing smoke that poisons the air
Tangible proof of cruel hate
White supremacy still reigns here
Oh, say does those gas bombs, cause long term infirmity?
On the freedom warriors brave and true
In the home of false realities.

21.
Freedom Baby What Will You Be?

Tangerine sized fist held high, you copy and repeat...
Chants of freedom, belting steady, from your chests heartbeat.
Beside mommy, beside daddy, holding big sister's hand. Growing
up in unrest, beginning to understand our collective demand.
Oh freedom baby, who will you be?
Will you be the one to set our people free?

Learning from the beginning, to poke out your chest, head held
high. Black Pride, Black Strength, Black Ancestral Breath, Black
Liberty nigh. Knowing things are wrong in the world, kids your age
dying by cops who lie. Afraid to tell anyone you fear you'll be next,
anxiety now consumes your play time...
Oh freedom baby, who will you be?
Will you be the one to set our people free?

My generation, middle age now, somewhat young and ready to
fight. Had a season of fictional ease, we grew up selfish, under
faux equality lies. But not you freedom baby, you are growing up
knowing, the battle has not yet been won. But not you courageous
little one, you will build community & never ever forget...
Oh freedom baby, I know what you'll be.
You'll be a great one, so much better than we!

Cause freedom baby, these are perilous times, as you look to us,
we look right back to you... Perfection of the Ancestors captured,
in your beautiful big bright eyes!
Ashe! Ashe! Ashe!

22.
FUCK THE POLICE

I never though it would be, that I would have to definitively say: Fuck the police! A freedom fighter and activist I've always been, but not this poignantly, not this focused... But then, you know "the when", I saw Mike Brown's blood boiling on the hot cement ground, awakening me to clear intention, clear revelation, clear permission...
So yes, I mean what I say, and yes I say what I mean.
With all my heart and soul, I say... FUCK THE POLICE!

It all finally clicked, no more sympathy, when I understood reality deeply. Systematically killing black bodies, covered by the lies of fearing imminent death. My people can't breathe, my people cant have skittles, or a cell phone in hand or pocket. Before a dirty filthy pig, with hatred of BLACK Skin, carelessly takes life as if it's nothing to them...
So yes, I am rightfully angry, won't pipe down, for white folks ease.
With all my heart and soul, I say... FUCK THE POLICE!

Do not quell us calm, until you help dismantle centuries old oppression. Shut the fuck up white folk, who dare lecture our grief, and how you'd prefer our expression. For far too long, we have lied to ourselves, thinking progress was laws and assimilation. Now many of us see, we'll have to agitate everything, until hate gets off our necks, so we can finally breathe...
So yes, I am in my warrior stance, Oya's winds all about me. With all my heart and soul, my tears from police terror that perpetually flow, let it be known I say: FUCK THE MUTHERFUCKIN' POLICE!

23
No Beginning, No Ending

Time shift shapes over me, but I remain the same.
Life goes on in the space before, in this space, in the space to
come. Remembrances of my future and shadows of my ancient
days tell me, my Love is my souls steady. I think I am just now,
but then I see that I am no surprise...

I open wide, I open wide, I open my EYE... And the other eyes
attract and repel to me, like a magnets law book of unanswered
knowing. I am here, I am there, I am with he, I am with she, I am
with none of the above... I AM a speck of God.

24.
A Black Jewess Lament

My Fanny Lou Hamer-isms expressed upon my face, every time a white Jew assumes I converted. I am ORIGINAL, it flows through my veins, my bloodline goes back to the actual tribes. Can you say the same? Mr. European... Mrs. European, I dare you to keep talking that smack behind my back... In your perfect world of non-melanin Hebraic-ness, as if it is 100% correct.

Sounds kind of *meshuggah*, doesn't? Not what you wanted to hear, right? That being BLACK and a Jew, is actually more natural than you, whose insults of hue, are overly trite... Ouch, did that hurt you? Hurt as bad as your prejudice and infantile branding of our ancient truths? This is what you do, have always done, and you know it's true... Fight me all you want, but you do! With your downcast eyes on me, I feel pressure to explain my lineage to you? Ugh!

Ethiopian Jew & African- American descent... I have plenty to say... I have seen and experienced it all! But what does it matter? What is it to you? Mr. and Mrs. European Jew... Do you really think *Moshe* had stringy hair and no color, like you? Oh, I know some of you have hair just like mine... Wanna know why, Mr. & Mrs. sly and talker of smack? It's because I'm ORIGINAL, you come from my Ancestors, and yes, they were BLACK!

I speak harshly to lament, to teach, to rectify a great wrong done for so long... Fire purification, to get all the dross out, no more of your bigoted nursery rhyme songs. A BLACK Jew in this world is not an anomaly, contradiction, or novelty you can hone.

I shouldn't have to feel I am not welcome in a synagogue, because of my dark skin tone deep... I shouldn't have to take on your European Ways, when my people kept the African ways enduring... I shouldn't have to be forced to rely on you to tell me, if

I am Jewish enough for your liking... Pushing me out, crowding me out, making me question the air that I breathe... Silly me! For your respect, for your acknowledgment, for you to stop your intrusive questioning... Oh, your fascism doesn't stop there, caste system of belief is always your thing. And if your a White Jew who doesn't do these things, than obviously, obviously, I'm not talking about you... But don't get too comfortable Mr. & Mrs. "Righteous White Jew", what is your record... What do you do?

Do you fight against the white supremacy among the Ashkenazim... In USA, In Israel, In occupied Palestine?

Or do you just allow silence to be your head-covering or *Tefillin*... Go ahead and answer... Answer and consider, but do it most heartfelt.

These rules made up, every single one... Making some Jews, no matter the hue, feel unholy and unwelcome... Like, your Talmudic hierarchies, things Torah never said... Telling us if we deviate an inch, we are not of Abraham. It's okay for the supposed most pious of European Descent, the *frum* and white, to Believe that a Messiah, a *Rebbe*, has already come a few different times... To y'all, that's alright, to y'all that seems true. It's also okay to still be considered a "Jew", if you're an Atheist or Agnostic, but here is where I get confused...

These wide accepted rules from the bowels of European Imaginings darkest... Trying to stay superior and in total domination, of the souls of those you oppress; purposely shunning. Your ways are not highest, stop shaming our holy space, so we can recall our ancient traditions, our ways...

Stop erasing who we've always been, and doing the violence of treating us less then human! Your greatest fear, white supremacy's biggest angst, is being erased; so you erase us presumptuously.

And while we're having this heart to heart, of regular and irregular heartbeats, I might as well ruffle all of your feathers, why not? You're so pissed right now, you can hardly breathe! Why such hostility? Such vitriol and angst? For any Jew, who believes Yeshua is the Messiah, The King? Your "holy frum" have picked Messiah's in the past, and were never excommunicated... Never told they no longer exist. Why can you so easily cast aside in this case? Casting off, birth right now null and void, in your supremacist opinion degrading?

Doubly hard on Black Jews who live in this Light, self-conscious, always having to feel obligated to shape-shift and perform, to your ideas of a Culture not rooted in you. But just like with anything else appropriated, you have pushed, to the very front, a theology that centers you and only you, Mr. And Mrs. white Jew.

Baruach atah Adonai Eloheinu Melech Ha Olam
My beautiful resonance saying these words, force you to hear the
Ancients sounding song.
Shema Yisrael, Adonai Eloheinu Adonai Echad.

Will you hear... Or are these words meaningless and of no consequence in your ears ? Will I hear, and stop allowing you to intimidate my place, my authenticity, my space? I lament the space to torment me, that I have allowed for so long... But no more! Truth rises in me, all around me, on solid ground I stand... You can't undo an ORIGINAL, you just simply can't.

25.
G-D In The Mirror

There is no contradictions in the bottomless.
I fell into a well, accidentally, when I was parched and wanted to cool my tongue. Head first, free falling, weightless... I glided fast and slow, harsh and easy... I heard a voice beckon me to open me eyes and see... I didn't want to, I didn't want to see, I didn't want to know. Soul knows, it always does... I knew more than I consciously let on.

And again, The VOICE said to me, "Open your eyes, dear one... Look and see, come on, see!" Again I refused... I just couldn't agree... I was afraid as I was falling; fast and slow, harsh and easy. And suddenly, a resin of roses and sandalwood began to express, and I felt at ease, at rest, at odds... Insecurity fleeting, not as uneasy, I opened my eyes and began laughing as I continued to fall freely...

It's only me, I thought to myself, mirrors all around with my image as I fall... How embarrassing the fear in me! I exclaimed aloud, why is this happening, what does this mean? I was so short of breath, as I continued my descent, never ending it seemed to be... The VOICE answered back, "what do you see?" Perplexed at the obvious, I answered... "It's just me!"

The VOICE then chuckled so loud I began to hit some sort of turbulence; journeying on- I began to see my image morph, or so it seemed, between me and a bright light, me and the Divine Glory! The moment it clicked in my hard-headed mind, the moment I understood what I was seeing... I was outside the well again, on solid ground, brain still reeling from the tumble; heart steady.

I had looked into the mirror, as I was falling freely down that well... Fast and slow, harsh and easy... And I found, what I know now, what I saw then... That there are no contradictions in the bottomless... I am a glimpse of G-D, and G-D is all of me... I looked in the eternal mirror, I thirst no more.

26.
You people Rhapsody
(White Proverbs in g Minor)

Why are you hurt? Why are you surprised?
Why are you quickly wiping tears from your blood shot eyes? Why
are you people always remembering? Why do your refuse to
forget? You people now have a Black President.. What else could
possibly be left?

I think you are just whiny, I didn't enslave you or yours...
I am so sick and tired of you talking equality, pulling that proverbial
race card. You live here in Amerikkka now, be grateful for it could
be way worse. You act like you people do not get special perks &
drain our countries resources.

So, maybe a few white people are racist, but you **b**lacks are just
as racist too. I reject the notion, I gotta go out my way, to respect
and acknowledge your "soul soreness."

I don't believe that you are oppressed, blah blah is your pathetic
songs tuning. You always cry foul, God only knows how, if you'd
try, maybe you'd be winning at life too!

Why are you people so unhappy? Lincoln freed your Ancestors,
don't you know? So what if black people, were never given
reparations, for their torture of heart and soul.

You say my advantage is my whiteness, I say you are a crock full
of shit! You should leave your children inheritance, then they'll
have advantages like white men.

How is it white peoples job to acknowledge, that you live in
ghettos with bad schools? Stop killing your own, the system works
fine, I've never had these problem like you.

Since I don't have these problems like you, listen to me now, they simply aren't true! Why should I spend my privileged time, weighed down by your case of the blues?

So, fix your own damn problems, who cares who caused your pain! Get over what we did to you: I feel absolutely no shame.

27.
Strong Black Coffee

Unapologetic for being who I am, is what my brew is filtered through. My potent flavors percolate vigorously in the pot of continual adversity; Pot is always on the fire, taken off at times, just to return...

Filter me some more; perfecting process, sure and steady and readying. Aromas intricately intoxicating, earthy addiction developing slowly. Best watch your intake, how you allow me to go down, blow before you sip, don't burn your tongue, now!

A little crème and sugar doesn't compromise my bold flavors, the holy hold of awakening! A little spice doesn't change the composition or the fact that; I AM a conduit of warmth and healing.

I am as ORIGINAL as *Buna Beans* can be, from the mountains, grand hall, and protesting in the streets!
Inhale me, Taste me, Drink my strong **B**LACK Coffee... And I promise, you'll never be the same.

28.
Pan African Hiccups

Indigestion cause' we've been eating lies for so long...
The good things, the choice things, creating air pockets in our guts
paths. Tricking us into to believing that we should turn back and
eat the fat... The bad parts, the disposable parts, because our
bodies are acclimated to the bad.

No one said it would be easy, though the taste was sweet as
honey at the first. No one said it wouldn't take getting use to, that
our gag reflex wouldn't activate at times. A little pain in uniting, a
little discomfort in seeing our way, a lot of frustration in those who
refuse to partake...

And then the hiccups, those annoying interferences... Trying to
stop our progress, so we'll lose heart... Come in like a flood,
distracting our steady resolve... Interrupting each breath & step we
take onward.

We have to gird ourselves with the strength and conviction of our
Ancestors Tears-Hopes-Dreams. We must keep on eating,
partaking, indulging in this good food that seems to not be
agreeing.

Washing all down with the sweet living waters, *Oshun* blessed,
abundance now found. So don't waste time being distracted by
these hiccups... Losing heart, solace, and strength.

Push yourself and push your neighbor with you... We need each
other, our breaths concurrent. After awhile, we'll be healthy and
whole, after a while we'll be sound.

29.
Assata's Mint Lemonade

I just want you to be free, Mama Assata, you are everything to so many you've never met. I just want you to be everywhere and anywhere your heart desires.

I sometimes imagine a scene, you and me, under a beautiful Baobab Tree... A tree older than the both of us... I bring a chair you sit in, under its seldom leaves... Please sit comfortably, you deserve it... All you've sacrificed, all you've offered...

This tree is old enough to tell us ancestral stories & requires we recall what we learn aloud. I sit at your feet, listening to every word and experience you want to share with me... You ask me to tell you of the storms and trials I have had to bear, my cup of wrath and glory. We weep, we mourn, we're angry, we laugh as we exchange life stories.

I pour you a glass of cool mint lemonade, that I brought for this day... Refreshing -Invigorating- Healing. I have some too... It's much needed. Our emotions have us quite undone, but we bask in its authenticity & release. You then sit down beside me on the ground, both our backs supported by the all knowing tree...

Freedom glowing- Freedom realized- Freedom being.
You drink your mint lemonade slowly, close your eyes, and smile embracing the suns warm blessing. I watch you intently, wondering what you're thinking, you notice, one eye opened and say to me:

"Girl, rest and relax, enjoy this breeze the Ancestors are blowing over our weary feet, it has been quite the journey, yes indeed!" She closes that slightly opened eye and returns to innocence...

Smile transfixed by peace, and I smile and start to take in all the beauty, all of the wind, this moment. She grabs my hand, so I can better understand, she holds my hand, as the Ancestors blow their breaths; The purest air we've ever breathed, and we're free, free at last.

30.
Obedience

Death of fear ruling my temple
I become brave in the *Listening*
I become uncompromising in the choosing
I adhere to the heights
I cling to the depths
I hear, I trust, I ACT
And that has made all the difference, yes it has!

31
Test Of Time

Steady as the hatred the world is filled with,
Is my G-D, my G-D to me.
Ups and downs, sideways and curved ways,
my G-D has never left me.

My G-D, MY G-D though seemingly forsaking me...
Hiding seemingly, to be found within me...
No, you have never left me.

My G-D, My G-D who seemingly has deceived me...
Many times seemingly... You needed me to learn to trust my soul
whispers earnestly, no matter the outcome or way...

Everything is unsettled, I AM still beefin' with you,
Yeah, I'm angry with you... The speck I AM, is YOU...
But it will be okay because your LOVE Divine lifts me high, even
when I'm fighting flight... My G-D, My G-D to me.

32.
Unbloomed

The desolation of solace, misplaced...
Where tribal connectivity should fill allotted space in heart
chamber. Waiting-Wishing-Needing-Wondering... To go, to stay,
to fly away?

A beautiful and unheard of: African Kadupul Flower is born, on
unsettled Amerikkkan soil... On unfamiliar grounds, bloom never
seen because she dies before dawn...
Yet, I resurrect and awaken the dawn with a song sweetly
scented... My love song...

My song of the hope I don't believe in, but that I need to come
true... I want to bloom in the light of day... I don't want the night to
be my story. I want to show the inward beauty that none have ever
seen, I want to live freely and be secure and not be picked lest I
not survive...

Secure in the unknowing, in the realization of continuity...
To be warmed by the SUN, nature change my flow... So the glow
can open me wholly... So I can leave this unfamiliar ground and
thrive holy & solely... I believe, this I know.

33.
Don't You Dare Cry

It was the final time... The final one... The last time I would let you make me hold back my cry. I cried... You hated that I cried... I don't apologize for it, my tears are the healing my being had been longing for.

Demanding I don't feel, show weakness.... Chastising my humanity, my fragility, my meekness. It is certainly to be understood, why I numbed out so early... All my years memories united in this reality, dark reality...

Like being taken advantage of by an older man, you took as me whoring, virginity snatched. You beat me, you cursed me, punched me out cold... Demanding I take it silently... "Don't you dare cry", you said to me, "Because you deserve this hurt from me!" I remember, and I bow in obeisance to the intense pain of this memory...

All memories collide, in and out... All united in this reality, before I found me. To the emotions and feelings I had to find again... To knowing I was more and not less... To know that my tears were holy & to be embraced... I inhaled and exhaled wholly in Ancestral entrancement.

Spirit walk work through the heat of the day, changing ways, learning my story, my ancient realities. Many tears, many tears... They flow freely, now... And at moments in time, I remember that you refused me this sanctity. I breathe and ask for help to navigate spiritually... And love you as I weep your presence, that needed to be separated from me...

My tears love you eternally.... I dare cry now, for you and me that just couldn't be realized... Just couldn't be.

34.
Seeing The INVISIBLE

Walk a little slower
Take a little more time to be
Chew completely, swishing drink, before swallowing
Make love passionately, intensely, as long as need be
Together or solitary, let go and be free!

Listen to the wind blowing against the shingles & the panes
Drink a hot cup of tea, blow intently, swiftly, shallow breaths
Entertain the floor creaks & strange rapping's & tapping's on the
front door.

Speak to SPIRIT... Listen-Listen-Listen: Breathe, return home.
Eyes focusing... Seeing more clearly, remembrance, one by one,
everything gently appears...

Everything I need is all around me, the unseen is part of my truest
reality. In the slowness of rampant steady... I see destiny- I see
yesterday- I see I'm ready.

35.
The Hunted

Jaywalking -Busted Tail Light-Walking-Breathing-Inquiring-Being. Death, right then and there, if your skin is gradient brown hued. Death, by killa' cop, if ORIGINAL runs through your veins steady and true.

Never will you, or I ,or they ,or she, or he who dawns mourning blessings on our dark skin... Whose hair rises to kiss the SUN; relentless hearts golden with all encompassing love... Never will we know, or want to know, the feel that the hunter gets before making the kill...

In hunting season, when it's perfectly fine to do, to kill without cause, me and you of brown hue... It could be he or she or me or you... Because we are the hunted-It's true! The weak have convinced us we are but prey, they did every evil thing to make it this way.

We are the grand prize, symbol of what they could never be or do... So their anger, led them to overcome their maker, their originator, their source in this realms quest. We are the hunted... You and me and he and she who bask in blessings beaming from G-D's holy face...

A refection of CREATOR in this time and space... They hunt G-D when their barrel is aimed in our face. They misplace a speck of unending time and space, every time our life force transcends from their anger & rage.

We are the hunted, remember our look, remember our face, remember or deep abiding pain. But wait til' the day... When the ONE who created us all culminates this order of things... And what will they do when they see us in that beautiful dark brown face?

What will you say, hunter?
Then, what will you say?

36.
Our Turn

Will we get it right?
Will we become more free?
Is all this pushing we're doing helping, no, like really?
Will we be able to get rid of the dirty &
greedy that stunt our collective journey?
Am I saying "Fuck The Police" in just the right timbre and tempo &
key? Will we finally get to revolution, no matter how hard,
bloody,ugly?
To everything we're spinning turn turn turn
This is our season of service turn turn turn
Are we doing every purpose for our people, under heaven?

37.
The Miseducation Of Forgiveness

Don't quell me calm, don't promise me "equality", if I'll forget what you are doing to me... To me, my Ancestors, my people, to those who will be... Stop killing me, because me is WE!

Stop telling ME that I need to forget all the harm, all the scars; you are not sorry. If you are not sorry, if you are not taking responsibility, how can two agree?

Yet you tell me, that forgiveness is a solo thing, that the Bible told you so, but in this you are lying & deceiving. You have to come to me, the me that is WE, and tell us that you are sorry... Turning from your evil folly.

But society cradled in white supremacy, tells African Energies, to ignore centuries of harm & storms... You say to us mockingly: "Forgive us if you're really civilized, grant us immunity, and hell no... We're not sorry!"

Yet we're so broken, we're so cast aside, we're wanting freedom so bad that we often compromise... Neglecting balanced and rightful pride, to be accepted by white haughty eyes... Human in inhumane eyes.

But they lie, they lie... Each and every time... We say they're absolved, they laugh in our faces. A little search of soul, to undo this perpetual trolling, from those whose hate depends on our low sense of self...

We die wholly and slowly every time, some of us tell the hateful whole, that they don't have to humble down. We die a little more each and every time, we don't demand that our hearts be allowed to grieve and be angry fully...Talking when we are ready, and in the time our soul deems is steady...

Hurting whispers... Lying frame.

38.
Talk Dirty In My Ear

My left, your right... The way sound has feeling as it warmly tickles... My left, your right, that's it, baby... Verbal intercourse, creativity, don't hold back from me...

Say it all, every bit, the things I wouldn't usually permit... Tell me, gently, aggressively... All or nothing, ALL OF IT! Talk me into an oblivion that makes the rest of me: My body loose control, spirit transcend, soul unbridled...

Who knew that soul to soul, could go deeply into the complexity of what happens when you talk dirty to me... Don't stop now, yeah you can tell me you love me, but make sure you mix that with holy naughty.

It shouldn't matter, when we dare, for truly I know you care, if I am letting you into this sacred solemnity. The way the winds from your mouth, gently blow on just that right spot, I'm loosing me into you truly...

It's okay to do, when you dare tell me what you're about to do... A nibble on my left, your right and I'm through... Ready to take flight, and I soar, you soar, we soar... We fly, we land... Um, Let's do it again.

39.
Mike & Marshawn

I

Prophesying your own death, yet didn't realize those bloody sheets you saw were for you... This haunts me in a way that is sad, enlightening... Meant to be. To a young man, everyone knew as Mike Mike... This prose is just for you.

Since August 09, 2014, your name, your life, your potential has filled my soul with fire. A righteous fire, that caused me to up my own ante... Radicalize and stand up to the systematic lies... For you and all of us... The Sons and Daughters of G-D, direct reflection of the image... Blackness, we are!

I dunno if you can see from where you are and travel, that your words have come true... Everyone does know you, just like you said we would. You are a breath of eternal flame that ignited us, challenged us, to fight for justice, in your wrongly executed name!

We will never forget you, no we'll never forget... Your pain, your dishonor, by disgusting pig slopping. No we'll never be the same, never be the same... And it's our honor!

So rest well young Ancestor, learn and glean from the great company your in. Know you have taught us so much, we know you are in the the winds blowing about us incessantly...

In rain, in hail, in sleet, in snow, in heat... The people gathered, the people disrupted, the people united...Your winds energizing us totally and holy... We can never forget.

I just want you to know, soul to soul, that you and I are connected, and I'm thankful.... May your winds continually blow... For change, for justice, for revolutionary love in action...

II

... And that it does... Yes it does! Over so many, especially the young... Like freedom Warrior Marshawn McCarrel, who just made purposeful journey to the Ancestral realm. Have y'all gotten acquainted yet? It's only been 3 days now since he took flight, to the highest height, of the unknown path, we on earth have yet to go. So, Let me tell you a little about who he is, it's important you know, it's important you know.

Just a few years older than you, when you laid on that ground for four hours and thirty minutes... He was one of the first to come from out of town... To come see that you got the justice you were do. Oh, he had already been dedicated to community for years... Cried many tears... Love of a thousand oceans deep.

In rain, in hail, in snow, in heat he cried out your name & the names of so many who had been slain... Doing the work, disrupting the status quo... His agony of soul, because of our collective woe. He loved so big, so wide and all knew... He was sincere.

But Mike Mike, let me tell ya', it's been so hard since you been gone... They hate us, they continue their slaughter and it's been killing us so deeply inside, though we try to stay strong. Wondering how we can make it, continue to breathe in this agony... So Marshawn, who journeyed where you are, a few days ago, decided that he had to indict the system by allowing his blood to flow...

He let go of his breaths and unsteadily steady heartbeat sounding... To arise more fight in us... More grit in us... To tell the system, to stop fucking with us! My heart is heavy, but I know y'all got so much to talk about and do... Where you are, sending gentle whispers of destiny to us... If we are still enough, we will hear... Your heartbeats in sync, forever in the other realm where peace can be reality.

But right now I cry... Been crying for 3 days now... Thinking about the oppression and trauma that took you both out... For the way that you both left this life... I hope you both know how loved you are... I know Marshawn will let you know all about everything we have been doing, to keep your name resounding...

So, rest powerfully you two... No more struggle, no more pain, no more wondering... We'll see you both at the first of the new dawns light... I can't wait... Til' then, we gonna be alright.

40.
Auras

Colors tell stories truer than our realest perception
You say you don't see color?
Than you don't see souls reflection.
Limitless intuitive, to do, to become,
life steadily unsteady and true...
Warmth of what to be or what to do...
The truth of inward groaning.

Mesh and mash, flowing from me to you, others, among blockage,
enlightenment. My colors speak truth, speak real, reveal all my
challenges & high tides; green and blue... And yes, yours too.

No matter how much I want to
pretend that I am strong or unbothered,
shifts in shadow reflection, tell no lies.

Here we go to and fro... Bumping colors and flow...
Unsteadiness of magnetic flow in this earth realm.
The above and below flow... flow... flow... Ready and brightening
vibrancy, love is my souls destination.

River of darkness free to shift and become... Whatever is needed,
whatever is supposed to be. Truth spectrum fully realized... Tell
my story, tell it to me... Remind me of time when I was completely
me... The part I am missing... Multicolored spectrum cast over
mahogany soul... Glow, bright, glow brighter!

41.
Draining Spirit

Unnerving, unending, unbending, deceiving
Unrelenting, unforgiving, unabated, demeaning
You never forget to set your clock to disturb me when I need to
be...

Focusing on my soul journey, and those I should be interlinked
with. If you really needed my help, if you really needed my
support...

I wouldn't mind, at any time, my hand &heart, lifting you high. But
you, have dark frequencies, that even I find hard to understand...
That merely want to distract me from following my life's plan.

I know you, I see you now... I will not allow this to be "our thing."
Figure out why your soul is sick and starving...
Maybe serenity will let you drain on her for a bit.

42.
Black Y. Goddess, Raped.

If it had only happened once, if I had only gotten away, if I had only realized what was happening to me... If I didn't have Stockholm Syndrome beckoning me, to drink another cup of doctored memory-

Then maybe, just maybe, I wouldn't have my EARNED doctorate degree, this expert view, this part of my story... It isn't an honor, I do not embrace the field study life dealt... The school set me back, way too costly, but I paid it off... I dealt with the debt!

Do not call me Doctor, do not bring attention to this pain that way, just listen, listen and learn. To have been taken in varied ways, I can recite my dissertation vividly, I hate it, but I do it to help others live!

Now that I have healed enough to allow memories, to be authentically as they are... I still shutter, I still hurt. This is forever... Forever I will have the scar. But you will never see, because it has transformed into a beauty mark... Until I tell you the origin, it seems to be something that has always been "pretty."

In flashes, in a twinkling of an eye, I stop breathing at certain moments in time... No one notices, they can't see, I have learned to force my breaths & regulate my irregular heartbeat...

I wish I had never earned this doctorate degree, in this field, but it is a part of me. I have to be responsible with this part of my story, and recite my dissertation to those who need it from me.

43.
The *Listening*

It took a while, to tap in just right...

To know what I was hearing, knowing how to distinguish it.

Making SPIRIT walk work a part of my every moment; second nature familiarity. It took time, it took focus, it took enclosing, it took denying; stimulated & intrigued by the ULTIMATE love drive-by...

The Listening- I can't imagine not consulting its beautifully composed score.

The Listening- It's more a part of me than fleeting feelings I indulge in erroneously.

The Listening- Warning, leading, guiding, teaching me homeward and onward.

The Listening- My internal GPS, i'll know the next step, when it's time to know.

44.
Sacred Circle Of WOMBMAN

No need to say, "This is just between us!"
The circle guards your soul like its theirs.
No need to ask, "Do y'all have my back?"
The circles support never slumbers or lacks.
No need to wonder,"Who can share my burdened heart?" The
circles heart is sewn into yours.
If you are blessed to be, in Divine agree...
With a circle of Black Wombman, who love you this deeply...
Never question that you are rich, far richer than most will ever
be... Never downplay this priceless wealth, in this season of
immense drought & perplexity.

45.
Sandy, Oh Sandy

Not one day goes by that I don't see your face in my minds eye... Sandy, Sandra, what they did to you happened to me in part, months before they stopped your heart. It hurts so bad that evil cops tried to soften your warrioress spirit stance, but you weren't having it...

You fought back! Standing up for what was right... I love you for that, but I hate that you had to die. They killed you, because you were BLACK, they killed you because you were rightfully proud... When cops dragged me out my car, I didn't fight them at the first... Did this save my life?

Hell, it doesn't even matter... Cause' you didn't do anything wrong Sandy, this hurts me more than I can say-You had every right to question, every right to demand those dirty cops treat you humane.

As I sat in a police car, for an air freshener I had hanging on my mirror. Being harassed, abused and much much more... I started to fight back... I couldn't hold it in anymore.

I see so many similarities between you and me, except I was finally let go, and they took your life savagely! Sandy, Oh sandy, I will never forget you, you are apart of me... The freedom work you were doing and wanted to do, will live through others like me. You are still speaking Sandy, we watch and tweet your videos often...

Calling out White supremacy and alerting the masses to get working... I wish you could be here with us sis, we'd love to have you fighting along with us still... Yet and still, you left us so much, your winds still blowing! Dear Ancestor to us you've become... We honor you Sandra Bland... We will never stop saying your name.

46.
KNOWING WHERE YOU DON'T BELONG

Don't tell me no bull shit about a "race card!"
Don't tell me our lived experiences are not real and all
encompassing. Ever since I was a little child, I knew there were
places I couldn't be... Safely.

It wasn't something anyone had to tell me, other BLACK Folk
know what I mean... It's the knowing before you walk in a place,
that the people there hate brown skin. Sometimes there are hints,
clues, key words and confederate flags waving loudly...
Sometimes it's the people who look at your arrival, like "Don't you
know this is whites only?"

Sometimes there isn't a clue, just a knowing, that " Nah, I don't
think they like black people here" sort of vibe consuming...
In 2015, at 32 years of age, this is still a reality, except it's so
normal that we often don't take it too seriously... I say we should,
we should definitely start taking it more seriously, pause & reflect
and acknowledge disparity.

We are so use to adjusting to systematic racism, and not it to us,
that we often do not give ourselves choices... Choices because
we're just trying to survive, but there is so much more we need,
we need FREEDOM! Freedom to simply be... Organizing efforts to
call them out, shut them completely down if need be...

Being able to tell white supremacy, it will not be able to be itself
peacefully... I don't blame you or me, who are beautifully draped in
BLACKNESS sweet... Cause sometimes, we just don't feel like
going through extra shit, and that's just the truth of it!

But this is our reality, we know the hate folks have deep in their
hearts; it's never hidden... We see it clearly! White folks will never
get it, unless they really truly want to see, they simply don't know

this reality...

They live above the rim where dunking doesn't include jumping...
Where walking is problem free, where their skin is a passport to
ease, oh and they get to breathe... Uninterrupted breaths,
whereas we're always reaching for an inhaler, that is often too
expensive for most of us to get.

47.
GOOSEBUMPS

You visited me in a way few will ever experience.
I wanted you to go away... Your presence was so strong.
Every hair on my arm raised higher than it could possibly go...

I couldn't see, my eyes closed, but I could feel the goosebumps
perplexing my very warm room. My arm hair tried to escape your
presence... I was so scared, I couldn't believe it was true. I
clenched my eyes tight, as you beckoned me to look at you...

I wouldn't, I couldn't, as you breathed warm on my body, you were
literally beside me... The same breath that breathed into me,
making me a living soul, a living being...

I asked you to back up, I was so scared of you... People think
they'd want this. But it was petrifying... Petrifying... Me and YOU!

You understood, my frail fears, loving me calm, speaking gently in
my ear. You are everything... You are my all. You came to see
about me, that's true love.

48.
HONEY BALM
(Dedicated to: *Sweet Honey In The Rock*)

Made in the earnest friction of care and musicality,
Honey Balm provides a thick healing layer over our wounds...
Spreading it on thick, keeping bacteria and infection at bay...
Giving us time to rest and become whole again, soul regeneration.
Scar being reduced in the process, when it's all said and done... It
will barely be seen, cause the honey balm coated it completely.
Every heart that hears it sing sweetly, the song to heal all
humanity.

49.
NINA'S HEART

Gave us all her heart and soul, but what was she given in return? Gave us revolutionary love, unbridled fire, all she wanted was to feel, have realized desire... A bit a warmth from infernos she started in everyone else, keep her safe and steady and whole.

No one gave her what she needed, tortured soul, giant genius, pushing truth, dying secretly. Abused, misused, neglectful, regretful... Beautifully human and broken and needful. I mourn that she lived to be used, and not one soul, could touch her in a way, to make all things new.

If she hadn't gotten her ass beat all the time, her classical piano dreams realized and thriving... Someone to see her as she is, without having to hide in compromise... Letting her rest; safety.

Would she maybe not have had, such a tragic demise? I wish I could undo what has been done. I wish she would've had more joy and newness. She has left us such a heritage in musical songs- I pause, I mourn, I remember, I'm resolved...

To learn from our Nina, that we must love our giant *Shero's* immensely, before there time on earth eclipses, this mistaken short-term reality.

50.
Orisha Flow

Oshun's sweet waters and Oya's warrioress winds blowing...
Colliding, crashing, causing a cyclone type storm.
They're fighting again, manifesting their collision in this earth
realm. Who will be the one to lead, who will be the head one?

Glittering Oshun is so sweet, but don't dare make her angry... She
can gush a wave dangerously... Peacock stance entrancing...
Yes, I said dangerously,dangerously, if need be.
Tumultuous the waters flow, as Oya's 9 rivers and winds blow...
Blessings and changes...Protectress of WOMBman, all her tumult
necessary, yes necessary; freedom awaits!

Can they just get along? Or will they fight and fight and not carry
out, the greater reality?

In concert they must be, because the GREAT ONE has deemed,
that they must share me... They are both needed. Their storm
washes over me... I realize, I allow what will be... What will be?
It's yet to be seen.

51.
Black Baby Doll

You can't have her, she is too pretty!
Look at her beautiful dark brown skin
Look at her beautiful big eyes, just like yours, just like mine
Look at her beautiful nose and face structure...
No, you can't have her... She's all mine!

These were the words of a mother, who understood...
That me, her daughter, would face a world that would tell her lies.
She hyped my understanding, to see that I was beautiful. By
telling me I couldn't have this beautiful BLACK Doll, and why...

She'd go on and on until she believed, I believed, that this BLACK
Doll was truly divine. Every time, for all the many many dolls of
mine... They had to be earned with staunch BLACK Pride! When I
finally won the game, no one could tell me that BLACK wasn't
beautiful- A knowing.

Throughout the years, I have had to deal with aspects of
oppressors lies... But I've never questioned BLACK is the most
beautiful prize, even in my temporal insecurities.
Truth lived... Sometimes dormant, but the Tree Of Life had it's
place in my inward forest... Simply because my mother, could see
ahead, BLACK Baby Doll used as amazing grace.

52.
BURN IT ALL DOWN NEXT TIME

Stop telling us to be peaceful, when that's all we do 98% of the time! Cause' when these white kids win football games, burning up shit, the world laughs, 100% of the time.

I've never heard Obama, tell them to be peaceful, after winning or losing the game... And we all know what they gonna' do... We all know they gonna' tear up shit like they always do!

But a few broken windows, over decades of time, for BLACK stolen lives, from racism brings us chastisement? We are literally fighting for our lives... For freedom to exist and to not be the hunted...

By racist ass cops and vigilantes that want us to bleed perpetually... But all we hear from those who are in "power" is: "Don't get out of hand-Don't be thugs-Be peaceful!"
It's maddening, so maddening... I'm so sick of it... When will it end?

Obama, on this you get the grade of a big fat F! But it's not just you, this grade has been earned by every BLACK "leader" throughout the K-land who could do something, anything to help, but still hasn't...

We're dying out here... DYING OUT HERE... Ain't no time to be politically correct! But were stuck with those who play overseer to massa', manipulating BLACK People who are oppressed... In bondage to differing chains and whips, throughout Amerikkka's blood soaked landscape.

Torture unending for all my kin in BLACK Skin, our greatest asset, and cause of our perpetual deaths. Fuck y'all for painting your progeny, your people, as violent animals who are not entitled to anger!

If these white folks can riot when they win or lose a stupid ball game, Why can't we riot when the system kills and Hates us- Hates us- Hates us, unending?! Why do you mourn things as if they have breaths, but BLACK People are told we're not worthy of our righteous vexation?

We haven't done much damage to your precious "things..." Only a few incidents here and there... Nothing really in comparison to our suffering. Yet, you lie on us in mainstream media and demean our righteous protests... It makes me so, so angry!

I wish we had done all you said we do, hell, BLACK People built this country from the bottom's bottom! Technically, you owe us for reparations past due... None of this shit belongs to you until your balance is undue!

Next time anyone wants to burn shit and loot, what if I yelled "Do it big, so the mainstream news can actually report something true!" But nah, I wouldn't ever tell you to do that, the risk is too high... The risk of your beautiful BLACK Life... Dead or facing life, because you broke a window, and the system wants to extinguish the speck of SOURCE you, I, represent.

Nah, I need you with me... With us... To plan how we gonna' get free for real, no matter the costs, plans strategic and whole... Whatever... Whatever... But whatever we decide to do, to pressure the power, we gotta be smart and stay alive to make the most impact!

We gotta take care of us... We gotta nurse our collective wounds... I don't know the answers to make it all better, but LOVE is something we can always do, as we figure out the rest... Figure our warrior stance...

It's up to us-It's up to us-
And not anybody, body else but us-
It's up to us- It's up to us-
It's up to you and me.

53.
Heartbroken Over Freedom

I'm tired of not being able to fully grasp what I need most...
What WE need most: Freedom... Freedom in a real, all
encompassing way. Not the escaping and zen-ing out "I'm free",
sort of thing... Not a semblance of inward freedom alone... But
authentically wholly, holy.

Can this ever be? When the environment we live in
is not an actual reality? Are we then really "totally free", or just
ignoring everything? Cause' that doesn't help you or me; not
really, not really, you see?

My soul, more than anything, wants BLACK People to stop having
to fight so hard just to BE. I've come to a very sad conclusion, I
can't have faith in hope... It is a distracting force that doesn't dry
my eyes, but if it dries yours...Go for it!

And I don't want to be equal with white folks, their bar is far too
low for my tastes... I don't want to oppress other people, destroy
other lands, as they've done the world. I desire to let my little light
shine... Gotta vibe-Gotta vibe-Gotta vibe highest.

All I know, is that we need so much more, but we have some
BLACK Folk, who want to hinder that flow... I am heartbroken and
yet I still rise everyday... I'm trying not to quit... Find a way to keep
going & flowing... It's so hard, so hard indeed, when it seems, we
will never get to *Freedom Land*... Yet I still have a dream...

I can't let go of the dream... Cause' Freedom is still my dream, my
song, my journey... Broken heart, cracks permanently fixed, soul
shines through... I-AM-LIGHT.

54.
Blood Song

CREATOR'S DNA spilled, all over this land
In the soil, on the pavement, in jail cells, in cops hands.

Who will atone for this carnage?
Who will pay the price for tortured souls?
When will the evil done for so long end? We need to know, we
need to know! When will the people stolen, from Africa's lands laid
bare, receive justice... Atonement, for all the blood spilled from
YOUR image bearers?

How long ,Oh, How long?
How long will you let this be?
Remember CREATOR, that's your DNA
Remember CREATOR, your ORIGINAL
Remember CREATOR, your blood cries from the soil
Remember CREATOR, YOUR blood spilling...

55.
The Point Of It All

Learning true pain, and overcoming it's sting.
Loving unabashedly, and having it end badly.
Becoming willing to share your truth, in all its authenticity...
The point of it all, is sacred remembrance.

What we once knew, what we were stripped of knowing.
So we could relearn, and choose to know it all again.
Filing our hearts, with fearless abandonment...
The point of it all, is sacred understanding.

Obeying Spirit, when you'd rather be comfortable.
Listening to soul clues, no matter how weird the making
vulnerable. Accepting the state your in, whatever that may be...
The point of it all, is sacred memory.

56.
Until Next Time

See, it's okay, you did your job with me... You just had to get me
here, that's all that was required. The CREATOR knew the rest,
he knew you could only do so much for me...

You loved me, but you just couldn't mother me like need be, but
it's alright... I get it, and I'm not angry. I will be sent everyone and
everything I need, don't worry about me... Seriously, I'm okay.

You deserve to be free... Free of your woes... Happiness and joy...
I hope you don't beat yourself up, I'm a survivor, I'm surviving still.
You did teach me to stand strong. I don't know if you even care,
but I need to make my heart known...

I have always loved you, and you'll always be in my soul...
This isn't the realm for us to be... But in the *Olam Ha-Ba* it will be
different... In the world to come, we will be able to be as we should
have been... Cause' we'll be whole then... Soul connected fully to
SOURCE; all things will be new.

Sorry we missed each other this time around, but certainly this
isn't the end... A new beginning will dawn, just not in this realms
hindrance.

57.
SPEAK TO THE GHOSTS

My job, before we walked into your house, was to speak to your ghosts...Whatever you had done, karmic manifestations of the evil, you channeled unease and unrest. I never felt this evil, maybe they listened to me, maybe it was you they wanted, for what you've done.

G-D protected me, I had no idea who you really were for so long... Speak to the ghosts? I get it now I think... Speak ease and comfort to the hell you created. My innocence, my youth, so blessed you didn't do it to me too... Your evil stole from me indirectly, you ruined your daughter, which took a mother away from me... You decided to make up for what you've done with gifts, gold, and unlimited funding... Speak to the ghosts?

When I got old enough to not want to do it anymore... SPIRIT telling me to soar, you hated me for it! I stopped speaking to your ghosts... You have to be haunted with them. You have to be tormented with them... They are not mine or hers or his... They are all yours... Handle them yourself!

58.
CLANDESTINE IDENTITIES

Sometimes I feel I don't know parts of me, well actually I don't really... So many secrets, so much silence, so much "hush, be quiet." I know my peoples origins, but I have been kept from my fathers side... They scared him away, though he begged to see me, they said no time and time again.

The natural ways I had from this other side, was always chided to get rid of and hide... But some things are so strong, that you can't deny... Music is how me and my fathers love survived.

How do I know? because I would always be told: "Ugh, you sound just like your father" when I would sing my continual bars and lines... Wouldn't allow me to play piano, because I guess that was his thing... Surprise, surprise! Glasses just like him, just a few things I hold and remember... In a blurry kind of memory... I seldom let it get too close to me, to feel the pain that may or may not exist... I'm just not sure.

African-American and a tad of Moroccan identity, a whole other family... I will always wonder... Damn, is this the non crazy side... Who would've actually loved & cared for me, rightly? It doesn't look like I'll ever know though, my mom would never give me the right info… I have a brother I don't even know... So she says, this shit is so crazy.

So to avoid impending travesty, I just avoid all high yella auburn heads around 14 years older or so... Don't want to accidentally date him, G-D that would be horrible! Don't even know his name... See how selfish the custody game is to the pawn, when one player cheats & refuses to show the score?

I will always wonder, about my dad, brother, aunts ,uncles, grandparents that I will never know... I will just have to allow all of what is for me, to manifest in it's timing... It's okay...I'm okay, It's gonna be alright... Cause' G-D is LIGHT and I'm a speck of it... This calms me, this assures me.

59.
TOKEN BLACK FRIEND

I refuse to ever again, be anyone's token BLACK Friend.
I have never meant to be, but being nice and naive, will
sometimes set you up in mess. Hasn't happened in years, but still
it's worth noting... I don't need this, you can keep it... Don't
deceive me, your full of shit!

You who like the idea of how "branching out" makes you feel...
You like how saying, "I'm not racist, I have a BLACK friend" feels
fluttering out your dry throat. You like being able to work your
micro-aggression's of BLACK People, under the guise of "I'm just
being honest", and "you're nothing like them" analogies and lies...

Decrepit soul, please, get away from me... I am not the one! I
know your kind now... You always give yourself away, it is so
easy. You usually approach me with some dim-witted
stereotype of what you think BLACK People are... Ask me if
random BLACK Folk in the room are related to me; cousins or
sisters... Cause we all look alike, right? I roll my eyes intensely,
hoping to journey into another realm where you can't find me.

Sometimes you don't come out with your token hunt rightly, but
eventually, you'll say you don't see color... Which means you can't
see, enough to actually be, a friend to me... Caught ya!

Chile' please, get away from me, before I cuss you out... I don't
want to be your token, your experiment, your person to ask a
thousand questions, just for your amusement in the error of
fetishizing BLACKNESS.

If you want to befriend BLACK People, fix your heart first, and
then test it... And stop acting like we're supposed to be your
human Google, on demand without question...

Chile' please, do you really think you are fooling me, or her, or him too? We know what you really want. You really don't want a BLACK Friend, you want absolution, and I for one, am not here for that... Shew!

60.
#TheMovementForBlackLives

We're breaking all of the rules, every single one
Freedom, the real kind is the goal... But some only want reform...
But reform being centered as the only, was not, is not, how it
started; not what many of us want...

The radical branch of the movement that is, often shut out by
those owned by the dollar! The real and true want revolution... At
least that's what I want, how about you? Who knew Mike Brown's
execution, would start this new wave of movement? It did, we're
here, we're fighting, it's hard!

So many against us, from Obama on down... Oh, I said his name,
some of y'all mad, but riddle me this... How can he be a supporter
of keeping BLACK People alive from cop terrorists... When he
never stops them, never makes effectual laws be at a try... Never-
Any- No type of fence to protect BLACK BODIES DYING... Blood
running in the streets coagulating.

I don't think reform can do much, but that is the realm he operates
in, do something! Do something, we're dying, do something! An
effort would have spoken volumes, no matter how far it would go...
A real fire of love, sweat of truth effort would have at least allowed
me to respect him... It's absolutely impossible now.

But we, the Daughters and Sons that have ORIGINAL flowing in
our veins, we're chided by Black Gatekeeper's, to be calm as we
die savagely, breaths hurting our chest as we end... Calling us
thugs, for losing our temper in brief spurts, justified hurt... A total
of a few minutes, over hundreds of years spanning...

But I am wrong for not wanting to pretend, that the first Black
President and others along with him, have committed this sin...
Always moving to save the world from all other problems but ours;

not worthy to them, not important to them, not enough to them, we are!

I refuse to pretend someone is for me, when they cosigned on an attempted murder decree in blue ink, I don't care what you blinded eye, rose colored glasses wearing, mofo's say to deny & absolve... We just have too many "respectable" knee-grows, helping white supremacy continue on...

Helping white supremacy maintain its reign... Playing this game over and over again... How can I lovingly help all of us, yes me included, to understand, that we need our Liberation, and not just a semblance of it?

How will we get free with all this dead weight trying to drown us? How will we get free with selfish ones taking advantage of visibility? I dunno, but the winds are strong, gotta give it our all, while things are moving intensely... Hoping we can get closer to the goal of dismantling this system entirely...

Can we? Will we? We have to at least try! Our progeny need to see and know we will fight for them, we will strive for them, we will even give up our lives for them!

I don't want them to ever feel the way I do right now... Abandoned by those who should be cradling us, as we move staunch and steady, our elders... Where are they hiding?

The ones, older and wise and seasoned with LOVE... In whom we can learn and trust... Please don't hide from us... Please let us know who you are!

Winds of change are blowing... Will we catch sail? Are we really ready? It doesn't matter really, the gale is currently raging...

61.
Brandon Jones, You are Worthy!

Your name is forgotten, not spoken among the litany of others...
Cause' some folks think one unarmed Black death by cop is more
important than another. That what you did, or who you are,
changes the speck of G-D that you occupy...

Brandon Jones, like others, you had a good heart, beloved in your
community, if only people would learn... The apple of your mama's
eye, she told me about you a few times... You, the life of any
party, you were solid and true to all you knew.

So yeah, Brandon, we realize you knew better, than to take things
from a store when it was closed, but I dare folks who justify your
death for this, to look at themselves a lil' closer...

If you ever cheated on your taxes, even just a little bit for gain... If
you ever illegally downloaded a song, instead of paying *Itunes* for
it rightly... If you ever went 10 miles over the speed limit, because
you were in a hurry that day... Or if you ever cheated on, an
important exam, because you didn't study to get that A...

If you have broken any rules, broken any laws, taken more than
you should, then how the hell, can you say with straight face...
That an unarmed Brandon Jones, deserved to breathe his last
breath?

Did you deserve to die by cops hand, when you download that
song or cheated on your taxes or exams?
Then why, do you cause his mama to question, if its okay for her
to mourn her son, her baby?

I bet so many of you "judges," have done so much worse than he
did... Yet you feel justified to act as Brandon's jury and judge...
Disrespecting the wonderful that he is and was...

Causing pain to sisters and brothers he left behind... His father, aunties, and special someones. Brandon, through your memory, your spirit, you are actually still living... Transitioned to the other realm... Where you can talk with the Ancestor-Elders... Learn and grow... Embraced and at home; safe.

In case you were wondering, if your name should live on...
Yes, Brandon Jones, yes you are worthy, worthy to be known!
Worthy to get justice, worthy to be respected... We are all human, in flesh, making mistakes all the time... We don't always do right... But no cop has the right to extinguish any of our lives.

Especially when we pose no threat and have a journey to make... What we were sent here to do, to learn, to be... Yes, you, Brandon Jones, you deserve to be remembered with respect. Because no matter what the "judges" say, your life matters, and yes I say this present tense... A mistake doesn't beget, an eternity of justifiable disrespect.

Along with a host of others killed, by the police terrorists in Cleveland... Yes, you took some cigs and bread... But how dare any of us ever think you deserved your death... Witnesses saw you calm and then, Wham, wham! That cop, BLACK cop, killed you dead... Extinguished greatness in the making... A missing thread in our collective tapestry.

You see, Brandon, white supremacy has henchmen that looks like me and you of brown hue... Even BLACK cops play the game... Often realizing way too late, that they are not seen as blue...

They still don't have privilege, like white cops do.

So, rest well young Ancestor, I am so sorry you had to leave your earth journey this way... We, who care, won't stop remembering you, fighting for you... We will set up holy solemnity for you... Brandon Jones, we won't stop, please know this is true, We won't stop saying your name.

62.
White Tears Hella' Salty

Got this big ole' cup of white tears... Washing down the white fears I'm chomping on... I have no more fucks to give. You mean to tell me, BLACK People are being killed, and you want to stop us from getting free? Co-opting our rallying cries; putting white or *all* where BLACK use to be...

What are you proving, but the point that you have way too much privilege and envy? Telling us, erroneously that "BLACK People are racist too..." Why is this your response, when the system is killing us, not you?

All these tears you cry, say you're a spoiled brat, who demands to be centered, you want your power and control to be unhindered... That's the real tea! You don't care about anyone else, always making everything about you. How about becoming a better human being... How many times have you shed tears for our slain? Exactly!

Yeah, this cup I got are your tears, you've only shed for you... And, I can only drink them moderately, cause they way too damn salty. Hypertension on your account? Hell nah, you're unworthy! But on the really real, I must solemnly admit, that they sho' is tasty!

63.
Nouvelle Négritude

Beautifully crafted by design... I hear my G-D calling...
I feel my Ancestors stirring... My **BLACKNESS** is not
a crime! It is the dawn of the morning, CREATOR has adorned us
splendidly; it is so. Enlightening, Entrancing,
fluidly Encapsulating my African Experience
in these Amerikkka's, in this supposed time frame...
On this leg of my freedom seeking journey. Inhaling all that is,
exhaling all that will be... I breathe... I fight... I stir...
I change the temperature...
Ashe'! Amayn! Aje'!

Afterword

Wow, so that was a lot huh? It was, it is, honesty... Honesty that reflects the times. I wrote this body of work with BLACK People, my people, in mind... I allowed the Black Experience in Amerikkka, through my lens, to allow the poetry offered here, space to be itself unbridled... Knowing that these offerings would touch my people deeply, allow healing to begin, to be that understanding friend who gets you... To make you think in a new way... To piss you off so much, that you will start affecting change immediately! *smile*

Sacrificing my own vulnerability & the surety, that many will totally misunderstand my intent, my heart, my LOVE... Loving you the readers enough to share me and you at the same time, in the literary space hanger of prose. How many times did you have that moment reading this offering, where what you have thought secretly, was given space and validity to be free and rotund? Yes, this is what I wanted for you, beloved.

I hope that everyone that partook of this poetic journey, followed my sincere request to not assume you knew the point I am making in each piece, until the end (see Introduction.) Life is messy and so is TRUTH... It slices right through things, exposing the contents to its sheath... That is why TRUTH purifies and allows transcendence... Transcendence is the goal! Being honest about myself and what I have experienced thus far, allows you safe passage to "go there", however you may need to, in your own life.

Were you challenged? Did you get angry with me? Did you cry? Did you feel Ancestral, Present, and Forever entangling in your soul? If yes, than this body of work has done its job... I am humbled and thank you for coming along with me... What is next for us? Oh, don't worry, this is only the beginning... You will hear again from me soon. Until we meet again on printed pages or device... Grow & LOVE.

Appendix

Organizations/Groups/ Individuals
Worth Our Consideration

Freedom Fighter/Political Prisoner: Joshua Williams (Ferguson)
https://www.facebook.com/Free-Joshua-Williams-NOW-997286490339173/?fref=ts

Black Autonomy Federation:
https://www.facebook.com/BlackAutonomyFederation/?fref=ts

Pursuing Our Dreams:
Facebook: https://www.facebook.com/PursuingOurDreams/?fref=ts
YouTube:
https://www.youtube.com/user/PursuingOurDreamsPOD

India Kager's (Police brutality Victim) Mother:
https://twitter.com/GinaBest

Sweet Honey In The Rock:
http://sweethoneyintherock.org/

Action Against Black Genocide:
https://www.facebook.com/aabg215/?fref=ts

Justice For Brandon Jones:
https://www.facebook.com/groups/468720959967245/

Remembering Marshawn McCarrel:
https://www.facebook.com/marshawn.mccarrel?fref=ts

Support Police Brutality Survivor: Antwynette Houston
https://www.gofundme.com/antwynettehouston

Lost Voices:
https://www.facebook.com/TheLostVoices/

Justice For Tamir Rice:
https://www.facebook.com/Justice.For.Tamir.Rice/?fref=ts

Justice For Tanisha Anderson:
https://www.facebook.com/JusticeforTanishaAndersonCleveland/?fref=ts

Follow me on Twitter: *@Empress_Orit* to inquire about the many other worthy individuals & group that need our support. Ashe'!

Glossary

Ha'aretz - Hebrew for "The Land." Referring to the Land of Israel/Palestine.

Buda - Amharic (Main language of Ethiopia) for "Someone with the evil eye, a witch, ECT.

Mushugga- Hebrew for "crazy."

Frum - Yiddish designation for European Ultra Orthodox Jewish lifestyle, that is very strict, minimal & complex.

The sh'ma- (Found in poem: Black Jewish Lament) is taken from Deuteronomy 6:4-9,and is staple prayer in Judaism:

Sh'ma Yisra'eil Adonai Eloheinu Adonai echad.
Hear, Israel, the Lord is our God, the Lord is One.
Barukh sheim k'vod malkhuto l'olam va'ed.
Blessed be the Name of His glorious kingdom for ever and ever.

Ashkenazim - Jews of European descent.

Rebbe - Yiddish word for Rabbi, which means teacher.

Buna Beans - Buna is how you say Coffee in Amharic, the originator of coffee.

Kadapul - Kadapul very rare, priceless flower that blooms at night, emits sweet smell, lasts a few hours, and then dies before dawn if it's picked.

MSM - Mainstream Media.

Freedom Land - African-American metaphor for BLACK Liberation, especially during Civil Rights Movement.

Olam Ha-Ba - Hebrew for "The end of the world."

Author Bio

ORIT is a Lover of G-D/ Freedom Fighter/ Poet/ Wordsmith/Healer/ Performing Artist (Singer-Actress-Dancer)/ Sarcasm Connoisseur/ Humor Enthusiast/among many other things. Uniquely of Pan-African (African-American and Ethiopian Jewish) descent, *ORIT* grew up in a small city in South Central Ohio, USA. After many years of cultivating experiences and travels all over, *ORIT* moved back to Ohio in recent times, and now resides outside of Columbus.

ORIT has been using words in every way possible to communicate messages since childhood. She not only writes them, but she is also a Multi-Lingual Orator and Spoken Word Artist, who can rouse & puncture hearts skillfully... When she wants to, that is. *ORIT* is a very down to earth person, and prefers using common & authentic language to communicate in ways that reminds everyone to level out ego, and embrace the hearth of the message. *ORIT* believes that the words, though important in their choosing, are only a reflection of the message...

"What a person remembers most will be what they take from your over all vibe as you speak words... The messages they decode from the unspoken weigh heavy... Did I convey the message wholly?"~ ORIT

ORIT has an extensive Theatre and overall performance background, and has been trained thoroughly in various ways and modes of being. She has starred or been Principle Dancer in many musicals and plays for most of her life. *ORIT* has also been singing since she was a child, and has had many opportunities to utilize and showcase this talent. *ORIT* is proficient in various types of music, and can sing in several languages. Her unique approach and natural style to vocalizing has been described as: "Deeply *Neo-Soulful* like a Negro Spiritual, with unexpected middle eastern styling's accenting."

ORIT is a veteran Dancer and choreographer that has encompassed all styles of dance; modern Dance being her base frame work. *ORIT* has also been chosen as Principle Dancer in many shows, and has competed to earn top accolades & distinctions in competition circuits in her earlier years. *ORIT* has choreographed for various events, and youth dance organizations as well.

ORIT has studied Theatre and Dance at top educational and conservatory institutions, but will tell you she developed mostly when she started to embrace working outside accepted framework and expectations. Though *ORIT* had taken a hiatus from performance to cultivate herself spiritually, she has been happy to re-embrace a part of herself that is innate to who she is in every way.

ORIT has spent a considerable amount of time in Israel/Palestine, and has a very accurate perspective about the levels of oppression non white people; particularly Black People face there. *ORIT* advocates every chance she is given for all Black Lives in "The Land" that are often not thought about, or are completely erased from mainstream consciousness and conversation. *ORIT* has been a Freedom Fighter since she was in second grade, and has helped support various situations and moments in liberation, in various places, over the years.

ORIT is currently an unconstrained Activist/ Freedom Fighter who has been heavily involved in the Movement for Black Lives... From Ferguson to Cleveland and a few other places in between. *ORIT* seeks to help the African Diaspora and the African Continent, to unite in unity, to fight systematic racism; one little step at time, one full breath in each moment... Then hopefully, maybe some leaps and flying when the climate permits.

ORIT has been immersed in various cultures throughout her life, which definitely enlightens her world view and love view. Though

ORIT is staunchly and unapologetically BLACK, her approachable and loving spirit is felt by all people of all backgrounds. *ORIT* wants it to be OVER-stood that she is a Lover firstly, who is very serious about restoring soul health to BLACK People, who are obtusely persecuted in Amerikkka and worldwide. *ORIT* does not hate any people, she hates white supremacy, and detests the police terror BLACK People worldwide are facing. It is important to distinguish that *ORIT's* passion, is fierce LOVE. Her love for her people is a reflection of herself, as she sees herself as irrevocably connected to her people.

ORIT has an all encompassing spirituality, that is the catalyst and guiding force in her life. *She* is not text book religious, in order to embrace deeper and deeper levels of spirituality and understanding. *ORIT's* passion in life is LOVE, Justice, The Arts and the FORCE THAT CIRCLES IT ALL... Giving to others and enjoying the winds... May they continue to blow!

Orif

AUTHOR
ACTRESS
DANCER
POET
SINGER
SONGWRITER
FREEDOM FIGHTER

www.ingramcontent.com/pod-product-compliance
Lightning Source LLC
Chambersburg PA
CBHW051838040426
42447CB00006B/594